# The World Through Bella's Eyes

## A Pit Bull's Story

# Peter and Lindsay Harrower

The World Through Bella's Eyes: a Pit Bull's Story

Cover design by Brian Courtright

ISBN 978-1-688210-49-3

# TABLE OF CONTENTS

# AFTERWORD

# ACKNOWLEDGEMENTS

# DEDICATION

This book is dedicated to every single Pit Bull and Pit Bull loving family in this world. For those who have chosen to rescue or adopt a Pittie, we say thank you and send blessings. Also, to every Pit Bull rescue organization we applaud your dedication and sacrifice to protecting this wonderful, misunderstood breed. We pray that Bella's story can help change even one negative stereotype, mindset, or misconception about Pit Bulls. If it does, we have succeeded.

We are most graciously thankful to our Lord and Savior, Jesus Christ, for inspiring Lindsay to rescue Bella and allowing our family to support, love, and protect the Pit Bull breed. Thank you for blessing us with the most amazing dog, Bella Louise, who we thank you for each and every day, and for entrusting us with sharing her story with the world.

# Introduction

## My Name is Bella

Hi. My name is Bella Louise Harrower. You can call me Bella, or Belly, or even Belle. I have a lot of names and I like them all, except when I hear "Bella Louise" or just "Louise." That means I did something I wasn't supposed to do. It's usually not a good thing if your parents holler your middle name—especially moms.

The reason I want to share my story is because I have seen and been through a lot—some bad, a lot good, and much of it about the struggles of being a Pit Bull. I'm so glad you're here, and if I could I would kiss your face because I love doing that!

A little background about me: I'm eight years old now. In dog years that's 56. I am what's known as a red-nosed Pit Bull and my fur color is pale brownish-red. Sometimes my daddy likes to call me a fawn, because he says I look like a deer.

Did you know that red-nosed Pit Bulls blush the same way humans do? When I'm upset or embarrassed, the skin around my eyes and ears turns pink. Strangers might not notice, but my mom and dad sure can tell.

My favorite things to do are to go for walks and hikes, or play with my mom and dad, chasing a ball or stick. I have learned lots of tricks from my parents like come, sit, shake paws, give high fives and high tens, give kisses, lie down, roll over, and I will even play dead! I love doing tricks because it means I get yummy treats.

My parents don't just give me dog treats though. This may sound kind of strange for a dog, but I like broccoli, cucumber, carrots, strawberries, and blueberries. I will pretty much eat any fruit or vegetable, except for lettuce. Lettuce is gross. It has no taste and it's like eating water.

I also love to sleep, and I don't like getting up in the morning at all. Sometimes my parents have to wake me up and drag me out of bed. I don't like when they do that. Sometimes they both leave the house and I am sad when they go. The only good thing is that I can go back to my comfy bed. It has the most wonderful soft blankets. Isn't it amazing how moms and dads know just what you like and need?

My parents love when I do zoomies. What's a zoomie you ask? A zoomie is when I run around as fast as I can in the same pattern. The best zoomie is when I race up the stairs, leap onto the bed, jump to the floor, then run back downstairs to the living room. I'll do this over and over again, at least six or seven times, sometimes more. Dad laughs and tries to chase me. Mom chuckles and shakes her head.

More than anything else I love to snuggle and lick. These are the best ways for me to show how much I care for and love my family.

The things I dislike the most are getting my nails trimmed, taking a bath, going outside in the rain, or when people get upset and talk loudly. Inside of me, I know it is my duty to protect and look out for humans, but when someone yells, I get confused and scared. My mom and dad say this is because of what happened to me when I was a puppy. Regardless of these few negatives, I know I have a good family and I have been blessed.

Often people say that Pit Bulls like me are not good dogs. Yes, I know we have been linked to dog fights and other bad stuff. But do you know Pitties are also called "Nanny Dogs," and back in the 1900s, we were displayed on military slogans and posters as one of America's most beloved breeds? Our primary job was to watch over kids and keep them safe.

Now when you hear "Pit Bull" a lot of folks get nervous. Some want nothing to do with us. When that happens, it hurts my feelings. Because of my large head and muscular body, I may look scary, but I'm not, I promise. I'm friendly and love to play and give kisses.

That's probably one of the things people might not like about me. I lick all the time. My mom likes it, but Dad doesn't. I don't know what his problem is. He's silly.

This is what I want you guys to know about me and my brothers and sisters. Because of some not-so-nice people who have done some not-so-nice things to us, good people are afraid of us. This is because those not-so-nice people taught us to do bad things.

The truth is Pitties are smart, reliable, and safe. Our instincts make us protective of our families. What we want more than anything is to say hello, play, and show how much we can love. If you give us a chance, maybe you'll get your face licked a couple dozen times. How does that hurt anyone? It might even tickle.

The story I'm going to share with you starts with what happened to me when I was just a little pup. I don't like to remember those times, but every now and then I have dreams that I'm still there. These flashbacks come and go, and I can't stop them. I just remind myself how wonderful my life is now, and that I have a mom and dad who love me and would never hurt me. Many of my brothers and sisters have been through similar situations, and I feel it's important for you to be aware. This is why I decided to tell my story.

It all began a long time ago, before I was named Bella. If I had a different name then, I don't remember it. Really, I think, I didn't have a name at all.

# CHAPTER ONE

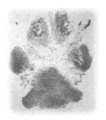

# I'm Sorry

I curl up in the corner at the back of my cage and close my eyes, trying to drown out the grunts and growls of other dogs, but the barking never really stops, even at night. Although I'm not asleep, I try to remember the dream I have sometimes of being warm with a belly full of milk, snuggled against little bodies that look like me, with my nose nuzzling into soft fur. I don't think that's ever really happened. It's just a dream.

One of the other dogs lets out a harsh yelp, loud enough to jar me into opening my eyes. Through the bars I can see him across the aisle in his cage. He's bigger than me and doesn't like me much. I don't understand why, but none of the other dogs here like me much.

Here in the barn where we live, each of us has our own cage. Because there isn't enough floor space, we're stacked on top of one another and piled so high that some cages reach the ceiling.

I get up to try to stretch my legs, but my spine hits the roof of my cage. None of us can fully stand up. Even the big ferocious dog across the aisle who's glaring at me now, is hunched over. At least when I'm locked in my cage and he's locked in his, he can't hurt me.

I wonder if his paws are raw from the wire floor, or if his claws are like daggers and curled in the way mine are. I think this is because I don't get to walk around outside my cage. If I could walk around more, scraping my claws against the ground would help keep them trimmed. I don't think my fur would be as patchy if my claws weren't like this either. I'm itchy all the time, and when I scratch, my talons either yank out my fur or cause knots, especially in the spots I scratch the most.

My first real memories here in my cage are of being cold. I could never get warm. Lately though, it's been hot and I pant all the time. Lots of us do. When it was cold, I didn't drink as much from the little bowl where the water goes. But now I'm always thirsty and the bowl has been empty since yesterday.

The odor in the barn is pretty bad, and I think the heat makes the smells worse. Through the bars I can see the puddles in the dirt. They come from the pee that runs down from the cages onto the floor. Sometimes the stench gets so awful, it's hard to breathe.

The big door at the end of the barn opens and for a moment, a cool breeze rushes in. I get closer to the bars to feel just a hint of it. At the same time the other dogs' barking picks up. It's loud enough to hurt my ears. Some of them thump against the walls of their cages with their tails or maybe it's their bodies. I'm not sure because I can't really see. Cage doors rattle as noses get pushed against them. The other dogs act crazy like this every time the man comes.

"All right, you dumb dogs, shut up!" he yells.

I watch the door close behind him, blocking out the breeze. He's a brawny man with big hands. As always he carries a bag and goes from cage to cage throwing a scoop of kibble from the bag in through the bars. He's careless though, and often pieces fall to the floor, into the puddles of pee.

The brawny man scares me sometimes. I don't think he likes me either, but I don't understand why. I try to be nice, wagging my tail to show that I want to be a good doggie for him. I've even tried to lick his hand when he gets close enough to the bars with the scooper.

Right now he's coming closer. And wait a minute, this is different. He stops at my cage and puts the bag down. Then he does something with the lock on the door. The next thing I know the bars swing away and the cage is open.

The man lets out a grunt and says, "Well, dog, you ready for the pits?"

I don't know what he means, but he reaches in and touches my head, then gives me a scratch behind the ear. He's never done that before, and oh! It sure feels good!

I wag my tail as hard as I can and lick his hand. I think this is what I'm supposed to do, and I think maybe he likes me after all. But then he yanks his arm upward, knocking me hard across the jaw.

My head slams into the wire wall and it hurts. I can't help it. I yelp and cower back to the farthest corner of my cage.

"Don't lick me, you stupid mutt," the man growls.

I don't understand what I did wrong. All I wanted to do was show my appreciation. But this is how he always is and it doesn't make sense to me. I've seen him do this to other dogs. Sometimes he's nice and will give a pet or a scratch, but then he'll let the dog out of their cage and kick it.

My cage door is still open, but I don't try to jump out. This is the only home I know, and even though it's cramped and makes my feet hurt, I am safe here.

The man leans over and picks up the bag. "You get two scoops today. You're gonna need it, 'cause later you're going to the pit," he says.

As he shovels food into my bowl, he starts to laugh. I'm not sure why, but I'm too hungry to care. I go for the food and chow down.

"See you later, you dumb dog," the man says.

I'm still eating as the door to my cage slams shut and the lock snaps closed. All I know is I must have done something right, because even though he hit me, he gave me lots of food—more food than he's ever put in my bowl before. For the first time I can remember, my belly is full. The feeling is almost as good as being in the dream snuggled with the puppies, and I think since I'm a little drowsy, if I take a nap I might just have that dream again.

I curl up and close and my eyes, and for once the constant barking doesn't bother me. Smiling, I begin to drift away.

A loud noise awakens me. Whether it's the slam of the big door, or the sudden frenzied barking and thumping, I'm not sure, but I get up and shuffle close enough to peer through the bars. The brawny man is back and this time he's not the only one.

I've seen this other man before—the skinny man. When he comes, they open some of the cages, put leashes on the dogs, and take them away. My questions are always the same: *Where are you taking them? Will I ever get taken away like that?*

"Get the bait," the brawny man says.

"That one?" the skinny man asks, pointing to me.

"Yes."

The skinny man opens my cage. He's got a heavy metal chain in his hands, the same kind they put on the other dogs when they take them. I bark because I'm not sure what to think.

"Shut up," the skinny man says, and he grabs me by the scruff.

*Ouch! That hurts!*

I can't do anything as he wraps the chain around my neck. Then he yanks hard, dragging me to the edge of the cage.

My cage is the third one up, so the drop to the floor is pretty high—too high for me to land on my feet. I tumble onto my side in the dirt, but already the skinny man is dragging me by the chain.

I do my best to scramble onto my sore paws and follow. It's not easy and he's pulling so hard. I don't know where he's taking me, except that we're going toward the big door. At first I dig my claws in to keep from going through, but he's stronger than me. He yanks, and I'm scared. I've never been on the other side of the door before.

Outside though, everything is bigger and different, and it's filled with new smells. The ground is mostly dirt like inside the barn, but part of this floor is covered with green stuff. I've never seen anything like it. I want to stop and get a good whiff, but the skinny man keeps dragging me.

He takes me into another building, and lots of people are here. I didn't know the world had so many people. Dogs are barking and growling here too, but I can't see them. It sounds like they're on the other side of the wall that's ahead of us, but I can't see over it. I smell human sweat and dog saliva, and I'm not sure what the other thing is, but I think... I think it's blood.

A dog begins to squeal, and all the people begin to holler and cheer. I look up at the skinny man. He's not paying attention to me. He's looking at what's happening beyond the wall where the dog is screeching.

That other dog's cries scare me and I try to tell the skinny man, *I'm sorry for whatever I did wrong. Whatever it is, I won't do it again. I promise. Just please take me back to my cage. Please! I beg you! I'm sorry!*

"All right, bait dog, it's your turn. Get in there and make us proud, you stupid mutt," the skinny man says.

He picks me up and drops me over the wall. I land with a thud and scramble to my feet. It's so loud and bright lights shine everywhere. My tail is between my legs because I'm nervous and afraid. I don't know what's going on. I don't know what I'm supposed to do.

Then in the other corner I see one of my brothers. I've never seen him before, but he looks sort of like me, except he's a lot bigger. I am so happy to see another dog, I wag my tail and start to scamper across the floor to get closer.

All of a sudden he barges toward me with his fangs bared. He plows right into me, knocks me over, and bites me in the side.

I yelp, because it hurts!

The crowd of people starts cheering and yelling. The big dog lets go, and I think for a split second he realizes his mistake—he didn't mean to bite me. I try to give him a slurp, to let him know I forgive him.

But then his teeth sink into me again. Harder this time.

I squeal and scream, and try to get away, but he keeps biting and thrashing me. The crowd roars with cheers and laughter. It seems like the louder I cry and struggle, the louder they get.

*Please stop! Please. I'm bleeding and it hurts. I'm just a little dog. I can't fight back against this bigger, older dog.*

"Get her! Take her down! Yeah!" somebody yells from the crowd.

The big dog doesn't care about my cries. He lunges for my face and latches onto my neck. There's nothing I can do except squirm under him and cry.

I don't know how long it goes on. All I know is it feels like forever. Finally the brawny man steps over the wall and makes the big dog get off me. I stumble toward the corner, limping. I'm shivering and scared, and there's nowhere I can go to hide.

"Come on, you stupid dog, let's go. You're done for the night."

The skinny man steps over the wall and puts the heavy metal collar on me, and it hurts because it digs into the place where the big dog bit me. He drags me back to the barn, grabs me around the ribs, and chucks me into my cage.

All I can do is curl up and do my best to lick my wounds. I hurt and ache all over. Many places on me are bleeding. This has been the worst day of my life.

I soon learn that it is only the beginning. Every time the door to the barn swings open and I hear the words, "Get the bait," I cower at the back of my cage, but it doesn't do any good. One of the men reaches in and grabs me anyway.

The days pass and the heat gets less and less. It begins to get cold again, and still the men come for me.

I don't understand why they take me to the pit so often and make other dogs hurt me. I don't understand why they keep picking on me, or why everyone hates me so much. I don't understand what I've done wrong. Whatever it is, I'm sorry. I'm so very, very sorry.

# CHAPTER TWO

# The Woods

I'm curled up in my cage trying to stay warm, when I hear the barn door. The other dogs bark and thump like they always do, and I do what I always do—cower in the back of my cage. I begin to shiver, but this time it's not because of the cold. From hearing his footsteps I can tell the brawny man is coming to get me again.

"Come here, you stupid dog. Get over here!" He opens the cage door and reaches in.

A growl starts in my throat. I want to bite him so badly, but only to protect myself. I can't though, because his big hand moves like lightning. He grabs me around the nose, clamping my jaw shut. I can't open my mouth, even to bark. The only noise I can make is a whimper, and I have to, because the way he's squeezing my jaw hurts! Something is different. He doesn't put the leash on me. Instead he carries me through the barn door. This time he doesn't go toward the building with all the people. He goes the opposite way to a parking lot. He takes me to a truck, opens the door, and tosses me in.

I land on the seat, banging into the passenger door. As quickly as I can, I scramble around to see what he's doing. He gets in the truck too, behind the steering wheel. Then he does something with a key and suddenly the seat underneath me starts to vibrate. The humming sound that goes with it is loud.

I've never been in a truck before, not that I can remember. We start to move and I'm not sure what to do. The one good thing is at least his big hand is no longer clamping my mouth shut. I can breathe and I can bark.

"Shut up!" he says, and he takes his hand off the wheel and holds it up like he's going to hit me.

I cower, getting as far away from him as I can.

"You stupid dog. You weren't good enough to draw a crowd. You're worthless to us. Now you get to find out what happens to worthless dogs."

I watch out the window, seeing the world as I've never seen it before. I didn't know everything was so big, or that the ground goes on forever and ever.

Buildings rush by and they look pretty—nothing like the dirty barn or the building with all the people.

After a while the truck begins to slow down. The brawny man pulls off to the side of the road and the humming vibrations stop. Through the window I see lots of trees, so many trees they all blend together. I think when trees are together like these, they're called woods.

"All right, dumb dog, get over here," the man says.

He reaches out and grabs me by the neck.

*Ouch!* I yelp, and he slaps me across the face.

"Shut up and don't move," he says. Then he starts wrapping a rope around my neck. This isn't like the chain leash. This is different, and he wraps it so tightly I can't breathe. I squirm, trying to resist, but I'm too small and he's too strong.

"Let's go. Over here," he says, dragging me by the rope across the seat, past the steering wheel, until I fall out onto the gravel shoulder of the road.

He doesn't give me a chance to get to my feet before he yanks on the rope. I sputter and cough, trying to breathe and stand up at the same time, but it's hard. I don't understand why he's so mean to me. I try to tell him again how sorry I am for whatever it was I did wrong. But he doesn't ever listen.

He pulls me up close to a tree, loops the rope around a low branch, and ties a knot. I try to rub my face and neck against the trunk to get the rope off, but it doesn't work, and the man left so little slack, it feels like I'm stuck against the tree.

"All right, dog, have fun out in the woods by yourself."

*What?* I don't know what he means. I look up at him, coughing again because it's so hard to breathe. I hope he can see by the pleading in my eyes that I just want him to take the rope off and take me back to my cage. I tell him I'll be good. I'll do what he wants.

His boot slams into my ribs.

I whimper and squeal, and sputter because I can't breathe. The man is already walking away. I try to bark, to tell him to come back, but he doesn't. He climbs in the truck and drives away, causing gravel from the shoulder of the road to fly up and hit me. I cry and screech as the little rocks pelt me, but it does no good. The brawny man is long gone.

Time passes slowly, and it's very cold here, much colder than the barn. All I can do is shiver against the tree and cough, trying to catch my breath. Every so often I try to bark, to call out in hopes that the man will hear me and come back, but it hurts to bark too much.

I can't really lie down because my head is so close to the tree, and it hurts standing on my frozen paws. Soon the sunlight fades and it's dark, and somehow it's even colder. All I can do is shiver and shake, and occasionally call out. I lean against the tree as best I can and close my eyes, just as little white flakes begin to fall from the sky.

Night turns to day and day to night again and the ground around me is now thick with white. I'm so tired, because I can't sleep trapped here like this. I'm freezing and can't stop shivering. My stomach aches, growling with hunger. Even though it hurts and makes it more difficult to breathe, every once in a while I find the energy to pull against the rope, hoping it will break and I can escape.

I've resolved that if I do escape, I'll figure out a way to get back to my home—my cage in the barn. I promise that I will try my best to be the dog that the men want me to be.

My efforts pulling on the rope, attempting to escape, are in vain. The only thing I've done is cause the rope to root more deeply into the skin around my neck and cut me. Beneath me the white ground has become slushy and red.

# CHAPTER THREE

# The Angel

I don't know how many days and nights I've been out in the woods, frightened and alone. Every day I stare down the road, hoping the truck will come back and the same thoughts come to me: *Why did the men leave me here? Why don't they want me anymore?*

I would have done anything for them. Even though I didn't like it, I did everything they asked of me. If only they would give me another chance, I'd be a good dog for them. I'd do better in the pit and not cry so much. I would be devoted and loyal, because I know deep down in my soul that's how I'm supposed to be.

The snow keeps falling and I can't stop shaking. My paws are frozen, my neck is bleeding, and I can't breathe. All I want to do is cuddle up in my cage, where I'll be warmer. And, although the food the

25

brawny man brought every day wasn't enough to fill me up, at least it was something. I am so terribly hungry.

I hear an engine that sounds like the truck and my ears perk up. I strain against the rope to get a better look. It is a truck, but not the same truck that the brawny man drives. It slows down and parks on the shoulder of the road.

A lady wearing a uniform gets out and starts toward me. She is young and pretty with dark hair and kind eyes, and for a moment I wonder if she'll be nice to me. But I'm not sure, so I hobble as far as I can behind the tree to hide. Since I can't see her, I'm sure she can't see me. But then she starts talking.

"Hi, little puppy. Don't be scared. I'm not going to hurt you. I just want to help you," she says.

Can I trust her? I don't know. I look up and see she has something in her hand—something that smells yummy. It's not much, just a morsel, but I can't resist. Slowly I creep out from my hiding place.

"That's it, sweet girl. Come on out. I just want to help you," the lady says.

I know I'm dirty and bloody and my breath probably smells bad, but it's only because I've been out here with nothing to eat for so long.

I inch closer and nip the morsel out of her fingers. And oh, it's so good!

*Oh, thank you, thank you!* I'm so excited, I try to lick her hand.

"Aw, you're a sweetheart," the lady says. She reaches into her coat pocket and then opens her hand. This time her whole palm is covered with treats.

"You poor thing. Let's get this nasty rope off of you," she says.

I gobble up the treats and barely notice when she slips a leash over my head. It's not like the heavy chain leashes the men use. This is soft, made of some kind of cloth. I try to lick her again to thank her for the food, but I can't really because her hands are on my neck. She's doing something with the rope.

Suddenly I can breathe again, and I'm not stuck against the tree! I can move!

The lady stands up, and I think maybe I should try to run away, or go around the tree where she can't hurt me.

"Come on, sweet girl. Let's get you out of here. I have more treats in my truck," she says, and she pulls on the leash a little bit.

This is much different than how the men did it. They yanked and dragged. The lady's tug is so light, I barely feel it. I start to walk next to her toward the truck, but it's hard. I'm weak and thirsty, and my paws hurt. I want to be strong, because I don't want her to get mad and hurt me. But I trip over my feet. I think I must look like a penguin, waddling and falling over.

I glance up to make sure she's not mad, and she looks down at me.

"Aw, I've got you, sweet girl," she says, bending down.

*Oh no! Oh no! I'm sorry, lady. I'll walk better. Please don't hurt me!* I plead, but I know she won't listen. I've learned in my life that people don't listen to dogs. The only thing I can do is tuck my tail between my legs and get low to the ground. Again I tell her, *I'm sorry. Please don't hurt me.*

"It's okay, sweet girl. It's okay. I'm just going to pick you up," she says.

What? She doesn't hit me? She doesn't kick me? She carries me to her truck and sets me down gently next to her in the front seat. She didn't throw me in. I can't believe she's helping me this way. Do people really do things like this? Is it even possible? I better lick her to show how much I appreciate her kindness. This time, since I'm not tied up, I go for her face. That's the best place to lick.

"Aw, so many kisses! Thank you, sweet girl. Now my whole right side is soaked with slobber," she says, but she's smiling. Then she frowns and mutters, "I don't understand what kind of monster would do this to such a sweet, innocent puppy. We're going to get you all the help you need, little one. Just be patient."

It's warm in her truck and the seat is soft and comfortable. As she drives, the vibration from the engine soothes me. I don't know exactly what this feeling of contentment inside of me is, but I think for the first time in my life, I feel truly safe.

I'm still tired and weak, and it hurts holding myself up, so I snuggle down into the warm seat and close my eyes. After a while, the lady stops driving. I perk my head up to see where we are. Outside is a building, and it's got big letters on it—SPCA.

The lady comes around to the passenger side and opens the door. She picks me up and carries me toward the building. Her arms are strong, and it's cozy being snuggled against her body. I think I like being held by the lady like this.

We go inside, and I hear lots of dogs barking. They're awfully loud, almost as loud as the dogs in the barn. She walks me down a hallway to a cage, but this one is nothing like the cage I used to have. This one is on the floor and it's so big I can walk around. It's also clean and neat with a little blue cot in the middle. The lady closes the gate and goes away, so I curl up on the cot. It's even softer than the seat in the truck, and I think I will be able to take a nice long nap. While I was in the woods I wasn't able to sleep, so I'm pretty tired.

Just as I close my eyes, the lady comes back. She comes into the cage and sets two bowls on the floor. One is full of water and the other has food. I hobble off the cot and go to the food. The whole time I chow down, the lady pets me. Nobody ever petted me that way before. It's nice.

"There you go, sweet girl," she says. "Now you'll start to feel better."

She's right. Already I feel much better. I eat every piece of food from the bowl, take a good long drink, and look up at her.

"I have another treat for you," she says, and she sets something on the cot that looks kind of like a log cut from a tree.

"Would you like a bone?" she asks.

*A bone?* I tilt my head because I've never seen a bone before. Carefully I move closer and sniff. It smells good, so I lick to see what it tastes like. It's good! All I want to do now is get cozy on the cot and chew on it, so that's what I do.

"There you go, sweet girl," the lady says.

She gives me a soft pet on the head, and gets up to leave. As she closes the gate, I look up from my bone. Compared to my old life in the tiny cage, this is like heaven. And I wonder, as I watch her walk away, if I just met a real live angel.

# CHAPTER FOUR

# My Girl

*What was that?* I hear voices—higher-pitched voices unlike any I've ever heard before. I'm in my new cage, resting on the blue cot, but I stand up and go to the gate for a closer look.

People are coming down the hallway, but they're not big like the men or the angel. They're miniature people. I've never seen miniature people before, and for some reason they're not as scary as the men. My tail begins to wag.

"Kids, don't get near that dog! It's a Pit Bull. They're dangerous!" a man calls out.

I see him coming up the hallway. He's a ways behind the kids, but catches up quickly. I back away from the gate, because he scares me, and I don't understand what he means. I'm not dangerous.

"Why are they dangerous, Dad? This one is cute." One of the kids stops in front of my cage and points to me.

"Because they are," the dad says. "They are a mean breed, known to hurt people. That one looks like a fighter. It even has blood on its neck."

"Where? I don't see any blood," the kid says.

"We're not getting a Pit Bull," the dad says. "Come on. Let's keep looking."

The dad takes the kid's arm to lead him away. The two other miniature humans follow. Soon I can't see them anymore, but I hear more voices coming. This time it's a man and a woman. I don't get near the gate because the man scares me, but the woman looks sort of like the angel, so I wag my tail a little.

"Look, honey, look at this one. It looks so sad," the woman says.

"Babe, that's a Pit Bull. We're not getting a Pit Bull," the man says. "Remember the other day, that story on the news about a Pit Bull attack? The last thing we need is a violent dog going after our neighbors."

"I guess you're right," the lady says.

"We need a less aggressive dog. I'm sure they have better dogs to choose from," the man tells her.

34

The man and woman keep going up the hallway and disappear, just like the miniature humans did.

I go back to my cot, and although I hear more voices, I don't care. Many people walk by, and if they look at me, it's just a glimpse before continuing on. I don't know what I did to make humans dislike me so much. But it's okay, because I don't know if I like humans very much either.

My eyes are closed when I sense someone standing at the gate to my cage. I open them and see a middle-aged, brunette lady staring. Even though she looks like she might be kind—like the angel—I'm still scared. She looks upset and I don't understand why. Was I bad? I've been here in my new cage, lying on the cot. I don't know what I did wrong.

"Lindsay!" the brunette lady calls out. "Lindsay, come look at this one."

I don't know why the lady is yelling, but I back away with my tail between my legs and curl up in the corner, as far away as I can get.

Another lady comes down the hall. This one is younger with blonde hair. She stares at me too, and says, "Oh my gosh, Mom, she's so skinny and dirty. And it looks like she has wounds."

"I know, Lindsay," the older lady says.

The young blonde lady has tears in her eyes. I don't understand why she has tears in her eyes.

"You want this dog, don't you?" the older lady asks.

"That's my puppy, Mom. And I think she's beautiful."

"What does the sign on the cage say?" the older lady asks.

"Pit Bull, beige, female, found in the woods. About six months old. Look how sad she is, and she's terrified."

Lindsay hunkers down in front of the gate. "It's okay, baby, I won't hurt you. Mom, can you go grab one of the attendants, please?"

The older lady walks away, while Lindsay stays by my cage. Soon though, the older lady is back with another lady wearing a uniform. Oh, it's the angel! I'm glad to see the angel again. My tail automatically wags.

Lindsay stops looking at me and stands up. "I want to adopt this dog," she tells the angel.

"That one?" the angel says. "She was brought in just a few hours ago."

"Do you know anything about her? What happened to her? Where does she come from?" the older woman asks.

The angel explains, "We found her tied to a tree in the woods and picked her up. We know nothing except a guess of her age, and that by her wounds and scars she's been abused. We believe someone abandoned her."

"What is wrong with people? Why would anyone do that to a dog? All dogs want to do is love us. Poor baby," Lindsay says and she sounds angry.

The angel continues, "I'm glad you're interested in adopting her. But, because she was just brought in, we have to hold her for at least 72 hours for safety and medical reasons. Our vet hasn't even had a chance to look her over yet."

"I understand. May I try petting her?"

"Of course, but I will warn you not to make any sudden movements. It's obvious she's afraid. And being abused as it appears she's been, she may not want the attention. If she growls, give her some space. Remember this is all new to her, and it's pretty evident she's been through a lot."

"I understand," Lindsay says.

The next thing I know the angel takes me to a different room with a bench. She sets me on the bench, and I curl up on the cushion. Then Lindsay and her mom come into the room, and Lindsay sits on the bench a few feet away from me.

"Come here, baby. It's okay. Don't be afraid. That's my girl," she says.

*My girl?* How am I her girl? I don't know what she means.

"Oh, Mom, she's so scared," Lindsay says next.

The older lady shakes her head. "Look at her tail and the way her head is tucked in. She's trying to shield herself from us. It's just awful what was done to her."

I want to trust these ladies, but I'm too frightened. I hop off the bench and go to the corner to get away from them. I feel much safer over here.

"Sorry, but I don't think she's ready for contact yet," the angel says. "Don't take it personally. She's just way too vulnerable right now."

"No, it's fine. I don't want to upset her anymore then she already is," Lindsay says. Then she turns to me. "Bye, baby. Don't worry, I'll be back and you can come home with me and be my girl."

# CHAPTER FIVE

# My New Mom

This morning I wake up after another long night in my new cage. I lay on the blue cot waiting to see what will happen today, and I wonder if more people will show up and walk past me?

I'm still here waiting when the angel comes down the hallway. She has come to visit me every day since I've been here. But today is different, because she puts a leash on me and says, "Let's go, sweet girl."

I don't know where we're going, but I like the angel. I follow her up the hallway and out to the lobby that she carried me through three days ago. That's when I see Lindsay, the pretty blonde lady who wanted to pet me. She's standing at the desk signing papers.

"Here you go, Lindsay," the angel says. "Here she is."

Lindsay smiles at me, bends down, and says, "Hello, puppy. I'm so happy to see you again. Oh my, you look so much better already. You truly are beautiful!"

Then the angel hands my leash to Lindsay and asks, "Have you had a dog before?"

"No. She's my first," Lindsay says.

"Just remember to be patient with her," the angel says. "I don't want to scare you, but dogs with backgrounds like hers will need time to warm up to you."

"Yes, I understand," Lindsay says. "Thank you for rescuing her and for all you've done to help her."

Then the angel lady asks, "Do you know what you're going to name her?"

"No, not yet. I have to figure that out." Lindsay looks at me again. "Are you ready to go, beautiful?"

Lindsay tugs on my leash, and I'm not sure what to do. *Why is she taking me? Who is she? Where are we going?* I think the angel knows I'm afraid, because she hunkers down next to me and pets my head. I try to give her kisses.

*Thank you, thank you!*

She laughs and wipes her cheek.

"So many kisses, my oh my," the angel says. "You weren't here long, sweet girl, but I'll miss you. Now you're going to your forever home. Be a good girl and take care of your new mom, okay?"

*Okay. But what does she mean? I never had a mom before. I don't even know what a mom is!*

# CHAPTER SIX

# Welcome Home

Lindsay, the blonde lady who is supposed to be my new mom, stops the car in front of a pretty house with a big yard covered with green.

She says, "Welcome home, beautiful. This is your new home now. You know what? I've just figured out what I'm going to name you—Bella, which means 'beautiful' in many languages. To me that's what you are—beautiful!"

She gets out of the car and takes my leash. I jump down and follow her up the sidewalk. I don't recognize this place. Everything is new to me and I'm scared walking behind this lady who's supposed to be my new mom. I think I'm supposed to trust her, and I hope I can, but I've never really been able to trust anybody before.

Slowly Lindsay moves through the yard and tells me to check things out. I'm not sure what to do, so I sort of follow. I step on the green stuff and it feels prickly on my paws and tickles my toes. This is weird. I have never felt anything like it.

There are a lot of new smells here. I sniff and sniff, trying to find a familiar scent, but I don't recognize anything. I don't know how I feel about this yet, but I think I'd better pee on this strange bushy object to mark my territory. Maybe that will make me more comfortable. Oh, this next funny thing over here, I'd better pee on it, too.

"Really, Bella?" my new mom says. "Do you have to pee again? That's like the third time now?"

Is she mad? I can't tell. But oh, what are those pretty, frilly things with leaves?

"Those are flowers," my new mom says. "Haven't you ever seen flowers before?"

I scamper over to them. Eww, they smell horrible and make me sneeze. I didn't expect that. It frightens me and I jump back.

My new mom laughs. "Oh, bless you, puppy. Did your own sneeze just scare you?"

I think, because my new mom is smiling, that maybe the flowers are okay. Slowly, I walk up to them again and sniff. And like the first time, they make me sneeze.

"Bless you again, puppy," my new mom says.

I don't know why she says that, but I know one thing. I don't like flowers. I bat at them with my paw, but it doesn't do any good. The best option is to pee on them. That will show them.

"Come on, puppy, you silly girl. Let's go inside," my new mom says.

I follow my new mom up the porch steps and through the door to this strange place. My tail is between my legs, and I think I'd like to find a corner where I can curl up into a ball and become as small as possible. I feel much safer that way.

"Look here, Bella. This is the kitchen and it's going to be your safe area for a little while, until you're more comfortable. See, I have it gated off for you. Over here is a comfy bed for you to sleep on. Your water and food bowls are here, next to the refrigerator. And this bin, right here, is full of bones and toys for you."

*Toys? What are toys?* I see all these new things and I'm a little overwhelmed, but I can tell my new mom is excited to show me everything. The bin with toys sure is interesting. The stuff inside is colorful and

I think I'd like to bury my nose in there and get a good whiff.

"Bella, do you want to play catch?" my new mom asks.

She takes a round thing out of the bin and holds it up. Then she squeezes it and it makes a funny noise. My ears perk up and my head tilts to the side. I'm not sure what that sound is.

"Here, puppy, go get the ball. Go get it," my new mom says.

She throws the round thing across the room, and I don't understand. I think my new mom is weird. I'd better stay where I am and keep my eyes on her.

"It's okay, puppy," she says next. "I'm sure you're not used to playing fetch. What if I throw the ball and we see if you can catch it? Are you ready, puppy? Here we go. Incoming!"

The ball flies up in the air and starts coming back down, and... *Ouch!* It hits me in the nose. I jump back, shaking my head.

"Oh no, I'm sorry, Bella. I'm so sorry. I just wanted to see if you could catch it," my new mom says as she gets up and comes toward me.

*I'm sorry! Don't hurt me!* I squeal and run away with my tail between my legs. There's a corner in this place where I can hide.

"It's okay, Bella. I won't hurt you. I just want to pet you and tell you I'm sorry," my new mom says.

I think she's going to hit me. But why? I didn't do anything. She's the one who threw the ball and bonked me on the nose. But she keeps saying the same things.

"It's okay, puppy. I just want to pet you. Don't be scared. Come here, Bella. It's okay."

I don't know if I can trust this lady. She looks nice and she smells nice. But not so long ago every person who came near me was mean. Now, it's hard for me to trust anyone. I know I should give my new mom a chance. After all she hasn't hurt me yet—minus the ball incident, but I guess I can let that slide.

I know that some people are nice. The people at the SPCA were nice, especially the angel. Maybe my new mom will be like her. She's still calling my name, telling me everything will be okay and I shouldn't be afraid.

I'm still unsure, but I've decided to take a chance and let her pet me a little bit—just a little bit though. If she does anything mean, I will let her know that I'm ready to defend myself. Slowly I creep toward her.

"Hi, puppy," she says.

She's not yelling. She's not making mean faces. Her voice isn't demanding or threatening. It's soft and tender.

"Aw, you finally came to me. There's nothing to be scared of here. I promise I will never hurt you."

She starts petting me. Wow. Oh wait. Now that feels good! Nobody has ever pet me this way before. I like this. Especially right above my tail, right there on my butt, in that spot I can't reach myself. That's got to be my new favorite scratching spot. Oh yeah. I'm loving it. My new mom can scratch me there any time she wants. From now on I think I'm going to call her the butt scratcher! Or maybe I'll just call her "Mom."

# CHAPTER SEVEN

# My Belly Girl

A few weeks have gone by now. The weird noises in my new home still scare me, and I'm nervous, but I'm starting to trust my mom a little more. She carries me around a lot, and every night she carries me up to her bedroom and puts me on the bed. It's strange trying to walk on this bouncy thing called a mattress. It feels funny beneath my paws. When my mom plops down next to me, sometimes it makes me tumble over. But since everything is soft, it doesn't hurt.

My mom laughs and says, "I'm sorry, Bella. I didn't mean to knock you down."

Every night she asks the same thing, "Bella, do you want to lie here next to me?"

Up until now, I've stayed on my side of the bed, but tonight, I inch my way nearer. She pets me, and I look at her. Her pets become fuller, and she adds in a few scratches. My eyes close because it sure feels good. Somehow I'm closer to her than I've ever been before. The next thing I know, she sort of picks me up, and draws me on top of her so that I'm lying across her stomach.

She keeps petting my head, and I lick her hand to show my appreciation. But I'm getting sleepy too, so I let my eyes close and try to relax. It's warm and cozy lying on top of my mom.

I'm still there, starting to doze off when I hear her whispery, tender voice: "I can't believe my puppy is finally letting me pet her like this. I feel like she finally trusts me. Do you trust me, Bella Louise? That's your full name—Bella Louise. Bella means 'beautiful' and Louise means 'protector.' Do you know you've lived here for a whole month now, Bella Louise? You look so peaceful lying here on my belly. Hey, that's what I'm going to nickname you—Belly, or even better, Belly Lou. We're finally cuddling, and that makes this an amazing, special moment. You are my girl—the best Belly Lou ever—and I promise to keep you safe and love you forever."

As I drift to sleep, my mom's words replay in my head, and she's right. It is a special moment. This is because I now know that I can trust her with my life. In return I make a solemn vow to protect and love her right back. After all, she's given me the perfect name— beautiful protector—which is exactly what deep down in my soul I know I'm supposed to be.

# CHAPTER EIGHT

# New Tricks

It's 9:00 a.m. on a Saturday and I bolt up onto the couch so I can see out the window. Somebody's here, but who is this guy? I don't like that he's walking toward my house. I'd better scare him away. I start barking loudly, but he keeps coming. He comes up the porch steps, and even though I know he's there, I can't see him anymore.

Then I hear a loud, *DING DONG!* It's another fairly new noise for me, and I don't like it, so I bark more and run back and forth from the window to the door.

"Bella, calm down. It's okay," my mom says.

*But Mom, there's a strange man on our porch and I need to protect you! You stand back and I'll scare him away. I got this. Don't worry!*

I keep leaping about and barking, louder than ever.

My mom doesn't listen to me. She grabs my collar to hold me still and opens the door.

The man standing on the porch says, "Hi, I'm Jackson, the dog trainer."

"Yes, hello. Come on in. I'm Lindsay," my mom says. "Shh, Bella, it's okay."

I'm confused because my mom doesn't seem to be afraid. I look at her, and then I look at this character named Jackson, and I'm not sure what to think. He's got gray hair, so he must be old, but he has a friendly smile and smells all right. I stop barking, sort of, but I'm still leery. I need to be, just in case my mom is making a mistake. Humans do that sometimes.

"Well, look who we have here," Jackson says as he eyes me up. "You're beautiful. What's your name?"

My mom chuckles. "Funny you said beautiful, because her name is Bella, which of course, means beautiful."

Jackson winks and holds out his hand for me to sniff. "Then it's the perfect name for her. Do you know Pit Bulls are my favorite breed, even though in my line of work I'm not supposed to have a favorite breed."

My mom tells him, "Bella's the first dog I've ever had. I'm still kind of new to this whole thing and learning as I go."

"Well, you've lucked out getting a Pit Bull then. They're known for their smarts and are a lot more intelligent than people give them credit for. They're also extremely loyal and protective of their families. They're active and strong, and make great working dogs, which means they like having purpose and responsibility. But on the flip side, they love being the center of attention and think they were intended to be lap dogs. Getting petted and snuggling is probably their favorite thing, even over food. I'll bet Bella's already proven how clever and manipulative she can be when she wants some loving."

"Wow. I didn't know any of that," my mom says. "But unfortunately, I haven't seen much of Bella's snuggly side. I've had her about a month and she only let me start petting her a few days ago. She's so scared and cautious about everything."

Jackson frowns. "Let me guess… she was abused?"

My mom nods. "You can see the scars on her face. The people at the shelter told me they believe she was used as a bait dog for dog fighting."

"Yeah, I see the scars," Jackson says. "Makes me angry."

"You and me both," my mom tells him.

"Well, she's lucky to have you now. So, you called me for training assistance. Is that what you'd like me to work on... her fear?"

"Yes, I think that would help a lot," my mom says.

"All right. Let's get started. Would you like a treat, Bella?"

Jackson takes something out of his pocket. It's not very big and I can't really see it, but I catch a whiff and it sure smells good. He tosses it in the air and I can't resist. I jump up and grab it, then chomp down. Oh my, it tastes as good as it smells!

"Good girl, Bella. That was a great catch," Jackson says, then he turns to my mom. "What I'd like to do next is take her through some situations and see how she responds. Then I'll explain what I want you to do to keep working with her. For now, if you wouldn't mind grabbing a seat to observe, that will keep her from being distracted by you, so I'll have her full attention. Sound good?"

"Sounds good," my mom echoes and she goes to sit on the couch.

I soon discover Jackson's pocket is overflowing with little morsels of yumminess. He says all sorts of new words to me, and when he says those words, I'm supposed to do specific things. As soon I do those things, he gives me another treat. I'm not sure if this is what it means to play a game, but if it is, then I like games. He teaches me to sit, wait, and come to him, and then we practice walking on a leash.

After a time, we walk over to my mom and Jackson tells me to sit. I do, and he tosses me another treat, just like I knew he would.

He says to my mom, "Lindsay, I have been a trainer for over 30 years, and I have to tell you, your pup is one of the smartest dogs I've ever worked with."

My mom grins proudly, so I do, too.

Jackson keeps talking. "But, you're also going to have your hands full. She'll know exactly what to do when she wants something, and she'll do her best to outsmart you. Right now, she might not be showing her true self, but that's only because she's still trying to figure you out. I can already see a bond developing between you, so I don't think it will take long. The most important thing is to give her purpose and keep her thinking and learning. She'll be a wonderful dog for you."

My mom chuckles. "She already is a wonderful dog. I took notes so I know what I'll need to work on."

My mom gets up and walks Jackson to the door. For a while they stand there, talking and thanking each other. This all seems silly to me. How much talking do humans need to do? Then Jackson turns to me. "See you, Bella. How about one more high-five before I go?"

I march right up to him and give the high-five he taught me. And wham!—out comes the treat from his pocket. I sure do love those treats!

"Good girl, Bella," my mom says, "Good girl."

I stare up at my mom and I think to myself, she needs some kisses. As soon as she finishes talking to Jackson and he leaves, that's exactly what I'm going to do—give her lots and lots of kisses!

# CHAPTER NINE

# My First Ice Cream Cone

*What's that noise, Mom? What is it?* I never heard that sound before. It's a jingling tune, ringing over and over again. I bolt to the couch and jump up to see out the window. There's a funny looking truck outside with pictures all over it, and people from the neighborhood are flocking to it. More kids are running up the road.

"Belle, what are you looking at, girl?" my mom asks as she comes over and peers out the window next to me. "Oh, now I see. And I have an idea. Come on, let's go."

She hurries off the couch and goes to the kitchen where she keeps my leash. I know before she brings it back that she has it. I can sense these things. Instantly I'm excited, wagging my tail and leaping about. I add in several barks to let her know how happy I am. I love when she gets my leash, because it means we're going out to do something fun.

*Mom, where are we going—a walk, a hike, maybe a car ride?*

We go out the front door and down the sidewalk toward the funny truck with jingling music. I wag my tail as we get closer, because there are lots of people from our neighborhood here. Since I've been living with my mom, I've met many of them, and I'm beginning to think there just might be more nice people in the world than mean people.

The lady who lives across the street says hello to me. She knows my name. A couple of the kids I've met say hello to me. We're standing with all these people and some give me a pet. I especially like pets from the kids. I still don't know what my mom is up to, waiting here by the funny truck, but that's okay. The kids in front of us are getting things from the truck—things that smell sweet and yummy.

I try to get a sniff at one of them, but the kid holding it turns away and says, "This is mine, silly Bella. Get your own."

*Bummer.* I look up at my mom expectantly, but she's not paying attention. She's looking at the pictures on the truck.

Finally it's our turn.

The lady in the truck leans out the window. "Hi, puppy. Aren't you beautiful? What's your name?"

I sit, because I think I'm supposed to, but keep wagging my tail for the lady.

"Her name's Bella," my mom says. "We'd like two vanilla cones please, one for me and one for Bella."

"What do you think, Bella?" the lady in the truck says. "Do you want an ice cream cone? You can only have vanilla because chocolate is like poison to dogs. It would make you very sick!"

*What's an ice cream cone? If it's the stuff the kids got, then yes, Mom, I want some.*

The lady from the truck hands my mom two things with lots of fluffy white goo on top—the same kind of goo the kids have. My mom leans down and holds the goo in front of my nose.

I take a tentative lick, and oh! This is good! It's cool and smooth, and I want more.

*Please gimme, gimme, gimme! This is good, Mom. Thank you, thank you, thank you!*

# CHAPTER TEN

# My First Bath

"Belly Lou," my mom says, "you are a smelly young lady. You haven't had a bath since you've been here, so I think it's time. Come on, follow me."

*Mom, where are we going? Upstairs? Okay. Let's play. I know, I'll find my bone and you can watch me chew it. That's always fun. Now, where did I leave that scrumptious thing? Oh, there it is—on the bedroom floor.*

I grab the bone, jump on the bed, and start chewing.

*Wait, Mom, why are you taking my bone away? Oh, I know, you want to play. You're going to throw it so I can chase it.*

I jump around, barking and spinning in circles. But why is she putting the bone up on the dresser? It's too high for me to reach up there. I'd better whimper so she knows I'm not happy about this.

"Quit your whining. Come on," Mom says. "Time to get clean."

*Whoa! Why are you picking me up?*

I don't mind though, because I like it when she carries me. I give her a good face lick to tell her how happy I am.

"Thanks, Belly, that's a lot of kisses," she says.

We go into the bathroom and she sets me down in the tub. Then she turns the knobs and water starts pouring out. I back away because that sound of all that water makes me nervous. I think it would be best for me to wait in the bedroom, bone or no bone. I leap out of the tub and high tail it out of the bathroom as fast as I can go.

As soon as I get settled on the bed, Mom comes in, and she's got a determined look on her face.

"Let's try this again," she says.

She picks me up and carries me right back to the bathroom.

"It's just water, Bella. It won't hurt you," she says, and she sets me down.

That noise is just too scary. The second she lets go of me, I bolt.

"Not again, Bella, come here, you silly dog!"

This time I don't get on the bed. I go to a corner where I can hide better, but Mom knows my hiding places. She comes over and picks me up.

This time when she gets me into the bathroom, right as she sets me down, she kicks at the door. I try to run, but the door slams and I plow into it, nose first.

*Ouch! That hurt!*

"Oh, Belly Lou." My mom sighs. "Are you okay?"

*No, Mom, I'm not okay. That water scares me, and you've got me penned in here. I don't like this at all!*

Maybe if I scoot in here as far behind the toilet as I can and curl up into a little ball, my mom will realize how afraid I am.

My plan doesn't work. She slinks in and picks me up again. She carries me to the tub and holds me out over the water.

"Here goes nothing," my mom says.

The next thing I know my feet are in the water— water that's warm and goes all the way up to my belly. I whimper, because I don't like this at all!

"Don't be sacred," my mom says. "It's just water."

It may be just water, but it's no fun the way she scoops it in a cup and dumps it over my back. The only thing I can do is shake to get it off.

"No!" my mom screeches. "Don't shake, Bella! You're getting water everywhere."

This being wet stuff is not fun. I shake again.

"Great!" my mom spouts, but then she chuckles. "Well, I guess we're both taking a bath today."

*That's right, Mom. It's only fair. You made me wet, so I'm getting you wet, too.*

At least that makes this whole bath thing bearable. She keeps pouring water on me, and then she scrubs me with soapy stuff that I think smells nasty, but she says smells good, and I shake as often as I can. Mom looks great with soapsuds in her hair.

I must say though, when she scrubs the soap into my fur, it feels really good, almost like a massage.

After that she starts in with the cups of water again.

Finally she says, "Good girl, we're all done. Let's dry you off. I have to dry me off, too. I think I'm more wet then you."

I jump out of the tub and she starts rubbing me with a towel.

"Aw, Bella, you smell terrific now!" she says.

I don't know about that, but I guess the whole bath thing wasn't so bad. I still feel funny though, and I need to run. Mom doesn't understand running is the best way for me to get dry.

Then Mom gets up. I'm not sure why at first, except she's heading for the door. She opens the door. It's the break I need. I burst right past her and race down the hallway.

*I'm free. I'm free!*

I shake and wiggle and sprint as fast as I can go— up the stairs, down the stairs. I jump on the couch, roll around, then rush back upstairs to do the same thing on the bed. Now this is grand! I bounce off the bed and repeat the whole thing.

Mom is standing at the top of the stairs, toweling her hair dry and grinning.

"Bella," she says, "you look like you're having fun, zooming all over the place. I think you've got a case of the zoomies!"

# CHAPTER ELEVEN

# Five Years Old

The years go by and all I can say is my mom is the best. I love her so much. She's a busy lady, going to work every day, but she always makes time for me in the evenings and on weekends. We go on a lot of walks, and hikes, and I have more toys than I know what to do with. Not only that, but she gives me tons of treats. Now that I'm five, which is about 35 in human years, I know plenty of tricks.

Whenever Mom invites people over, or we go to visit my grandmother—we call her "Gammy"—I show off. I get a lot of praises, pets, and scratches when I show off. My mom's praises and pets, however, are the ones I like best. She and I are the perfect team.

It's a lazy Saturday morning, and as usual Mom and I wrestle around, being goofy. She scratches my chest and it feels good. But then she hits a spot in my armpit and yikes! I can't help it. I yelp.

My mom yanks her hand away. "Bella, what did I do? I'm sorry," she says.

My mom would never intentionally hurt me. She's looking at me and I can tell by her expression, she's worried.

Lightly her fingers trail over me to the place under my arm. "What is this, Bella? You have a bump that isn't supposed to be here. I don't like this. I think, maybe we should go to the vet."

A couple days later, Mom comes home from work early and gets my leash right away.

*Are we going for a car ride?*

We are. I know because Mom leads me to the driveway and opens the passenger door. I'm not sure where we're going, but I don't care. I love car rides.

She puts the window down just enough for me to get a cool breeze. I open my mouth and pant, and it's heavenly.

All too soon though, she pulls into a parking lot and turns the engine off. Then she hooks my leash on again, and I jump out. We start toward the building, but when we get to the entrance, I freeze. We don't come to this place very often, maybe once a year, but I recognize it. I don't like it here at all. I turn in my tracks and start back toward the car.

"No, Bella, we have to go in," my mom says. "Everything will be okay."

I'm not strong enough to pull my mom away, so I have no choice but to go with her. Inside, behind the counter, is a woman dressed in white.

My mom tells her, "This is Bella. We have an appointment. She has a bump on her left side, behind her front leg. I was giving her a scratch and she cried when I touched her there."

The lady tells us to have a seat and the doctor will be out shortly. It doesn't take long. We follow the doctor into a small room, and my mom picks me up and puts me on the table.

The doctor looks at the bump under my arm and says, "I'd like to do a needle biopsy. That's where we pull some tissue out of the lump with a syringe. I'll be able to look at it under a microscope, and we'll know right away whether the cells are normal."

I feel helpless and unsure, and I don't like the skinny, pointy thing the doctor picks up. I know what it is—a needle. That's because every year when we come here I get shots. Today my mom stays right beside me, talking and singing to me, because she knows it calms me down. I feel the poke by my arm. It hurts, so I try to back away, but my mom holds me still. It's okay though. After being with my mom for five years, I know if I just stay focused on her, she won't let anyone hurt me, so that's what I do. I look at my mom and listen to her soft singing voice.

The prick of the needle ends as quickly as it began, and the doctor leaves. Mom and I stay in the room by ourselves until he comes back.

"Lindsay," the doctor says, "unfortunately there's no easy way to tell you this. The lump under Bella's arm is what's known as a mast cell tumor. It's cancer."

"Oh no," my mom says and her eyes fill with tears.

The doctor continues, "Pitties are usually pretty healthy dogs, but tumors like this are also fairly common in the breed. We can do surgery here to remove it, however, because of the location being under her arm, I am concerned about being able to remove the whole tumor. There is a possibility that she might not have use of her leg in the future."

"Okay," my mom says. She's still teary. "When do we do the surgery?"

"Before we go ahead, I'd like Bella to see another veterinarian for a second opinion. We also need to run more tests to make sure the cancer isn't anywhere else.

There is a specialist a little over an hour from here who may have some suggestions on the best way to proceed. This type of cancer can grow rapidly, so I recommend making that appointment as soon as possible."

My mom says, "I will call today."

# CHAPTER TWELVE

# Car Rides

"Bella, are you ready for a little road trip?" my mom asks. I'm in my spot in the passenger seat of the car, and she reaches over to pet my head. Then she says, "If you're good, I'll buy you a special treat afterwards."

*Did you just say treat, Mom?*

I tilt my head and wag my tail.

"You're so smart. You know exactly what I mean when I say treat. The question is do you want an ice cream cone or chicken nuggets?"

I wag my tail and tilt my head farther. *Ice cream or chicken nuggets? They both sound great to me!*

"Okay, we'll get nuggets," she says.

Mom opens the window just the right amount and since we have to go on the highway, the breeze is strong, the way I like it best.

Soon we arrive at a place I've never been to. I can tell by the smell though, that's it like the other place I don't like so much—the one with the doctor and needles. My mom talks to the lady behind the counter, and we sit in the waiting room.

Eventually a man in a white coat comes out and says, "Bella? We're ready for you."

My mom gets up, shakes the man's hand, and tells him her name is Lindsay. Then she introduces me.

"I'm Doctor Gordon," the man says. "Come on back."

We go into a little room and my mom picks me up and puts me on the table, just like at the other place.

"I'm really worried," she says to the doctor.

The doctor looks at the bump under my arm and says, "First thing we need to do is take Bella to the back room for some scans."

"Okay," my mom says. "Bella, you be a good girl. They won't hurt you, I promise."

She puts me on the floor and hands my leash to the doctor. I don't want to go with this strange man and leave my mom behind. I whimper and struggle to get back to my mom, but the doctor picks me up and doesn't give me a choice. All I can do is stare at my mom until the door closes and I can't see her anymore.

My mom is right about one thing. The scans aren't that bad. It's kind of like when Mom wants to take pictures of me, and she tells me to wait and stay still. I have to do the same thing for the scans.

The best part is when the doctor takes me back to my mom. She picks me up, and I lick her face because I'm so happy to be with her again. The doctor tells us to wait while he reviews the x-rays, and he'll be back.

I don't know how long we wait, but it's a while. When finally he comes back, he doesn't smile. "Unfortunately, I have bad news. Bella's x-rays show numerous spots. I'm very sorry."

My mom tears up. "Is there any way to help her?" she asks.

"We'd have to start with the surgery to remove the tumor. After that we're looking at more tests to determine the extent of the cancer. Depending upon what we find, it could mean additional surgery as well as on-going medication and treatments."

"I understand," my mom says.

"I know this is a lot to take in right now, and I don't want to pile more on, but if you decide to go ahead with everything, there will be significant costs involved."

"How much are we talking about?" my mom asks.

"With surgery and treatments, a rough estimate would be around $5,000."

"That much!" my mom's eyes fill with tears again.

"Would you like to take the weekend to think about whether you want to proceed? You can give me a call on Monday and let me know what you decide."

"What happens if we do nothing? How long does Bella have?"

"That's hard to say. My best guess would be a few months to less than a year."

"She's only five years old," my mom blurts, and then she blinks and says, "Yes, I'll take the weekend to think about it."

We get back in the car and Mom swipes at her eyes. "You were such a good girl in there, Bella. Are you ready for those chicken nuggets?"

I wag my tail and whine a little because I can't wait, and my mom smiles through her tears.

My mom goes through a drive-through, and the man in the window hands her a bag. I don't need her to tell me what's in there. My nose already knows.

"Relax, Bella," my mom says, and she laughs because I'm whining and bouncing in the seat.

Chicken nuggets sure are tasty!

It's not long before the bag is empty and we're on the highway.

My mom says, "We have a lot of praying to do this weekend, Bella. We need God to heal you."

# CHAPTER THIRTEEN

## It's a Miracle

All weekend my mom is upset. She prays over and over, each time asking God to heal me. I think her prayers are about the weird lump behind my leg. I do my best to reassure her by giving kisses and licking away her tears. I'm not worried about me. I'm worried about her. She saved my life and gave me the best home a dog could ever have. My job now is to love her back as best I know how by being her beautiful protector. That also means helping her feel better when she's unhappy.

Monday morning comes and she says, "Bella, do you want to go for another long car ride?"

I bark and spin in circles.

*Where are we going? On a hike? I love hikes. But it doesn't really matter. Anywhere is fine with me, as long as I'm with you!*

My mom chuckles and says, "Okay, okay, I hear you. Let me get your leash."

We get in the car and my mom puts her hands on the steering wheel, but she doesn't start the engine right away. I can sense the same troubles that plagued her through the weekend. She looks over at me and smiles sadly. Then she bows her head and talks quietly, "Dear God, I know I have been praying this whole weekend. But please, please help my dog. She has been by my side all these years, and she has helped me more than anyone knows. She has protected me and kept me safe when I needed it. She makes me laugh and smile with all of the crazy stuff she does. She is a bundle of joy and such a good girl. I wish people would understand that Pit Bulls are not bad dogs. They are wonderful dogs. My Bella proves it.

"Lord, I know the doctors will do their best to fix her. Look at her, sitting here next to me with her tongue hanging out. She's so happy and so innocent. She has no idea what's about to happen to her. Please help me to make the right decisions, and no matter what, help her get through it all. Thank you, Lord. Amen."

She starts the car and off we go. I'm just happy to be with my mom, going on another road trip. I love sitting next to her and being her copilot. She's so nice to me and treats me so well. I just want her to be happy and proud of me.

"Belle?" she says after we've been driving for a while.

I tilt my head. *Yes, Mom?*

"Do you know how much Momma loves you? I promise you that everything will be okay, and you just need to trust me, like I am trusting God."

I know what that word "love" means now. I know because my mom tells me she loves me all the time. I tell her, *Of course I will do whatever you say, Mom, because I love you, too!*

I'd hoped we were going on a hike, but we arrive back at the same place we were last week—Dr. Gordon's office. We're taken into the little room, and like before, my mom picks me up and puts me on the table.

Dr. Gordon asks, "How are you doing today, Lindsay?"

"Not great, honestly," my mom tells him. "I'm nervous about my girl."

"I know, but we'll do our best to take care of her." Then the doctor turns to me and asks, "How are you, Bella?"

I have to jump a little to give him a lick in the face to let him know I'm all right.

He pets me and says, "Thank you for those kisses. You're a smart one, aren't you?"

That calls for another jump and lick.

Doctor Gordon laughs, and that's good, because so does my mom. Then the doctor says, "Guess I don't have to take a shower after work. Bella took care of that for me."

"I'm sorry, Dr. Gordon. She's a licker."

"It's all right. I don't mind. Dogs bark and lick— that's how they show us they care. She's a special girl," the doctor says. "Now, I know you've decided to go ahead with the surgery today."

"Yes," my mom says. "It's an expensive procedure, but I'm trusting God will make a way. What's most important is helping my Bella."

The doctor smiles and says, "Before we get started, I'd like to get another round of scans, okay?"

I get taken to the back room for pictures again. This time I don't mind because I know what to expect, and more importantly I'll be seeing my mom again soon.

Afterwards, like before, my mom and I wait in the room by ourselves for a while. Eventually the doctor comes back. I can smell something different about him. He's not as sad as he was before. He may even be excited.

"Lindsay," he says, "I have Bella's x-rays here. I must say I have never seen anything like this. Let me show you."

He holds up two funny looking pictures under the light and continues, "This is Bella's scan from Friday. Do you see the spots we talked about?"

"Yes," my mom says.

"Now, look at the scan from today. Do you see the difference?"

"No spots," my mom says.

"That's right." Doctor Gordon nods. "Now, I want to run a few more tests, and we shouldn't get our hopes up too much, but if what this scan is showing is accurate, the only cancer in Bella's body is the tumor under her leg."

My mom whispers, "Oh, thank you, God, for hearing my prayers." Then she raises her voice. "Thank you, Doctor. I don't know what else to say."

"Neither do I," Doctor Gordan exclaims. "It's a miracle!"

# CHAPTER FOURTEEN

# Surgery

"Belly girl," my mom says as she hugs me and kisses my head. "I need you to be strong for Momma. Be a good girl and listen to the doctors and nurses while they're trying to help you. I'm so sorry I have to leave you here. You have no idea how much I'm going to miss you. But God will protect us both, and I know you will be okay."

*Wait a minute! I already had pictures taken. Why did you hand my leash to the doctor again? Mom, why are you walking away? Why are you leaving me? Are you forgetting me?*

I whine and cry, but she doesn't come back. The nurse who came in with the doctor is holding me and won't let go. She doesn't understand I need to be with my mom.

*Mom! Momma!*

The nurse takes me away, and after that the last thing I remember is lying on a cold table and falling asleep. When I wake up, I'm in a crate. It's not much bigger than the crate I lived in when I was a puppy. The only difference is that this one is neat and clean, and I can stand up all the way. But I'm scared and I want my mom. Where is she?

I cry and whine, not because my leg and chest hurt, but because I don't know where I am, and I don't know where my mom is. The nurse hears me and comes to the crate.

"Hi, Bella," she says. "You're going to be okay. You just need to stay still and rest. Your momma will be here to see you tomorrow."

I lie down because I'm tired, and my leg and chest really do hurt a lot. I close my eyes and eventually drift off.

In the morning, the nurse comes and takes me out of the crate. She brings me to a new room—a much bigger room, sort of like the cage at the SPCA. My leg and chest don't hurt as much as they did before. The ache I feel is in my heart. The nurse told me my mom will be here today, but I'm afraid I'll never see her again. This is the worst feeling in the world.

I'm here in the big cage for a while, when I hear the door open and footsteps come down the hallway. I don't look up because I'm sure it's just the nurse. She's nice, but she's not my mom.

But then something trickles past my nose. I lift up my head. It's a scent I know well—*Mom!* I jump up and rush to the gate and there she is, coming down the hallway with the nurse.

I am so excited, all I want to do is break through the gate and run to her. I want to leap into her arms and kiss her face over and over again. She didn't forget me. She's here!

The nurse opens the gate and Mom comes in. She drops to her knees and gives me a hug. In return I get in as many licks as I can.

"Oh, Bella Louise," she says, "I missed you so much! Are you ready to go home?"

*Oh, yes, I'm ready. I may be tired and a little stiff, but nothing will make me happier than to be home with you, Mom.*

At home, my mom won't allow me to walk, jump, play, or do much at all. She keeps telling me to lie down and stay. Really, I don't mind. It hurts walking on my sore leg. The only thing that upsets me is when Mom won't let me sleep in our bed. She says I have to sleep in my crate. She explains that it's for my own good, and that I need to stay quiet so I can heal. I understand all that, but I still wish I could sleep with her. I sleep best when I'm with my mom.

A week goes by and I feel much better, so when Mom asks if I want to go for a car ride, I'm ready! The ride is great, until we stop and park. I know exactly where we are—Doctor Gordon's office. My fear is that Mom will leave me here again.

Once we're in the examination room, my mom tells Doctor Gordon, "Bella's doing great. She's a real trooper!"

"I have good news for you as well," Doctor Gordon says. "Bella's surgery was a success. We got the whole tumor and she is cancer free."

My mom is so happy she jumps up and down. I think she learned that from me. She's hugging and kissing me, and squeezing. I don't get it, really, but I sure like all the attention. It's kind of hard, with Mom holding me this tightly, to get in some licks, but I do my best.

"Bella, are you ready to go?" my mom asks. She's crying again, but this time they're happy tears. "On our way home we're going to stop and celebrate. Do you know what that means?"

*No. What?*

"It means today you don't have to choose. I'm going to get you an ice cream cone *and* chicken nuggets. What do you have to say about that?"

I lean over and give her my best cheek slurp—the real slobbery kind. That's what I have to say about that!

# CHAPTER FIFTEEN

## Share the Love

A couple of years have passed since my cancer scare, and Mom and I have a pretty solid routine. I'm 7 years old now. That's 49 in dog years. This morning Mom went to church, which means it's Sunday. Now I'm waiting for her to come home, lying on the couch like I usually do. She seems to be taking a lot longer than normal today. It's already getting dark outside.

I hear a car go down the street, so I pick my head up just enough to glimpse out the window, but it's not Mom. A few minutes later I hear another car. I think maybe there are two cars, one behind the other. Before I have a chance to look, I hear the garage door open. Mom's home!

I get excited and run to the kitchen, barking and wagging my tail. I can't help it. I'm always excited when she comes home. Sometimes Mom is kind of slow getting out of the car. I don't know why.

Today though, I hear the car door shut, but it's not the only one. My head tilts curiously. Now I hear another voice—a man's voice and I don't recognize it. Somebody is out in the garage with Mom! I bark more so she knows I'm here, ready to protect her from this stranger.

Mom opens the door. "Hi, Bella," she says.

I do my thing, wiggling and wagging my butt, and barking, letting her know how glad I am that she's home. Then I see the man—he's right behind her. He's kind of tall—taller than Mom, and he has a beard.

"Bella," Mom says, "This is my friend, Peter. Peter, this is my crazy dog, Bella Louise."

I get close and sniff. He smells all right, but I'm still cautious. Making sure my mom is safe is my number one priority.

I don't leave Mom's side all evening, keeping a close eye on this Peter fellow. They eat dinner at the kitchen island together, and then sit on the couch talking for a long time.

After a while I decide to see how this guy will react to me. I go over to him and let him pet me. He seems like a strong guy, and I like the way he touches my head. It feels good.

*Oh, wait, what are you doing to my ears, Peter? Wow! That feels amazing. Nobody ever pets my ears like that. Please don't stop, keep going, keep going!*

He stops anyway, but it felt so good I need to return the favor. I jump up onto his lap and lie down on top of him. I'm trying to be nice, but I also hope he'll pet my ears again.

"Aw," my mom says, "she likes you."

*Well no, Mom, I'm not 100% sure about him yet, but I think maybe he's okay. I guess you could say he's growing on me.*

It's pretty late when Peter finally leaves. I soon figure out this is just the beginning of Peter becoming part of our lives. Peter comes to our house a lot, and the more he's here, the more I like him. Mom likes him. I know because when he's with us, she's always smiling. We go on a lot of walks and hikes and car rides together. He gives me treats when I listen well, and he seems to like throwing balls for me to chase. I certainly don't mind that. It's my favorite game.

With the exception of my uncle and my grandpa, who we call "Pap," there aren't too many men I trust around my Mom, but I'm beginning to trust Peter. I have heard him tell my mom he loves her. I've heard her say she loves him, too. Because of my mom saying those words to me, I know how special they are.

# CHAPTER SIXTEEN

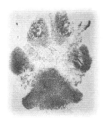

## Happily Ever After

"Are you ready, Bella?" My mom asks. She bends over to adjust my special collar. It's got poufy, different colored flowers all the way around. As she stands up again, she says, "You look so pretty, Belly girl."

If I could talk like a human I would tell her the same thing. She's the pretty one, wearing the long, lacy white dress. She doesn't have flowers around her neck like me though. She's holding hers in her hand, and her flowers are real flowers, not pretend ones like mine. That's okay with me, since I'm not a big fan of real flowers.

It's a beautiful day and we're at a lovely park. My mom hands the leash to my young cousin Teagan and asks if she's ready, too.

Teagan nods.

"Is it time?" Pap asks. He looks handsome as well, dressed in a black suit with a bright blue shirt.

"I think so," my mom says.

We can hear music playing as we make our way along the path. Ahead of us many people are seated in chairs that are set up in rows. Between the chairs is an aisle, and at the other end of it Peter is waiting.

"You go first, Teagan," my mom says. "Go to Peter, Bella."

My cousin Teagan leads me up the aisle, dropping flower petals out of the basket she's carrying. I don't care so much about those, because I have a much more important task.

We get to the end of the aisle where Peter is. He's dressed up in a light gray suit and is more handsome than I've ever seen him before. He hunkers down and makes the signal for me to give him a high-five.

I do the high-five and he whispers, "Good girl."

*I wasn't doing a trick because you asked me to,* I tell him. *That high-five was me giving you permission to marry my mom. Just remember, my mom is my number one, and I'm watching you, pal.*

That's me posturing. What can I say? It's a dog thing. I don't need to watch Peter. I know he loves my mom and me both. I'm actually really glad that after today I get to call him "Dad." I will have a dad, and not just any dad, but a really awesome dad!

After the wedding, Mom and Dad go away for what feels like an eternity on something called a honeymoon. It's not so bad for me though, because I get to stay in my house with my favorite dog sitter, Ms. Stephanie. I'm always on my best behavior for her.

When my parents finally come home, I'm so happy to see them I jump up and kiss them both as much as I can. I wiggle and my tail thumps away. Ms. Stephanie is great. She spoils me, and I like her a lot, but she's not my mom and dad. I missed them so much!

Eventually things settle down. My mom and dad have unpacking to do. I get to watch, and then my dad takes me out to the backyard to throw balls for me to chase, and the three of us have a splendid evening.

At bedtime though, something is different. My dad doesn't leave and go back to his house. He gets in bed on my side of the bed, taking up my space. I scramble up and nose my way to where I normally sleep, trying to push him out of the way.

Mom laughs. Then Dad laughs. I don't get it.

Mom says, "Bella, you're going to have to learn to share."

*Yeah, well, I suppose. That's what you think, Mom.*

I soon find out, after a couple nights of this, that my dad is a real bed hog.

Honestly, I don't mind. There really is nothing better than cuddling with both my parents.

The other bonus to having Dad live with Mom and me is that most days he works from home. That means I'm not alone all day anymore. It also means I can't snooze the day away. I have a job to do—protecting my dad while he works. I have found the perfect spot to do that, right in front of his desk. Sometimes I get too comfortable and doze off, but don't tell him that.

Every once in a while I remember what my life was like as a pup. At that time I could have never imagined I would be so fortunate or have such a perfect home. Now I know, without a doubt, I'm one lucky dog. You could even say I'm the luckiest Pit Bull in the world!

# Afterword

Imagine you're in a room you've never been in before and it's dark. The only light comes from one tiny night light. That night light will help you to see where you're going.

My parent's goal is to add more light to that dark room by sharing stories like mine.

Would you like to help, too? What if you treat someone nicely, even though they were mean to you? Could it be that they just had a bad day? How about listening to your parents when they ask you to do something that maybe you don't enjoy, but you do it anyway?

Could you share a story of something that happened to you that at the time wasn't great, but you learned a lot from the experience?

Here's an example: My dad hates picking up my doggie droppings in the backyard. He has to pick them up before he mows the lawn. If he doesn't, it's going to make a big mess. Ewww. He always tells Mom how nasty it is. She just laughs and says he's doing a great job. From my place on the comfy chair next to Mom, I smile and wag my tail, telling him the same thing.

The point is, even though he hates it, he does it, because it's important to keep our yard nice and clean, and because he loves me.

The more we do for others, the more light will be turned on in that dark room. Gradually the world will become brighter, and before you know it, you'll be able to see everything clearly.

Now that you have learned about my life, I hope you understand that even though I'm a Pit Bull, I'm not a bad dog. I don't want to hurt people like everybody thinks I do. I'm protective of my family, and especially kids, but it's only because I care about them.

Like me, my Pittie brothers and sisters are not bad dogs. Many of us have had bad owners who've hurt us and forced us to do bad things. All we want is to make our parents happy, which means if our parents tell us to do bad things, we'll do them. Please don't hold this against us. After all we're just dogs. We do what we're told, trying to please those who feed and care for us. We don't know any better.

Do you know there are some cities in the United States that have banned Pit Bulls? That means none of us are allowed to live there. Over 900 cities have labeled me and my brothers and sisters too dangerous for people to be near. It's not fair and it's wrong.

If you ask me, that "dangerous" label belongs with the people who hurt and mistreat us. They are the real problem. Those people should be held responsible for the choices they make, and for teaching us to do harmful things.

I was not born a monster or a killer. I was born to give love, and share love with the people around me. I want to lick your face until you're soaking wet. I want to curl up on your lap and be close to you. I want to play catch with you, or run around the yard with you chasing squirrels. I want to help you in the garden by digging holes for your plants. You use a shovel. I use my paws. I want kids around me to snuggle with and watch over. I love my family more than I love myself. These are the natural instincts of a Pit Bull.

It's important not to judge dogs before you get to know them. Just because a Great Dane is big doesn't mean it's not friendly. Great Danes are one of the biggest breeds of dog in the world and they are very nice.

Pit Bulls might look scary and tough, but we deserve love just like every other dog. Do you ever wonder if words like "dangerous" hurt our feelings? They do.

Many of us have similar stories to mine—stories of overcoming abuse to become the protective, loving, and loyal pups our instincts tell us to be.

Please don't be afraid next time you see a Pit Bull like me. Ask questions if you want. It's okay. Try learning more about our breed before you decide you don't like us. If you're lucky when you meet one of my brothers or sisters, you'll get licked until you're soaking wet and giggling because it tickles. Then you will see how big and scary we really are.

Do you know I have a cousin named Tyson who's also a Pit Bull? He's a blue-nosed Pit and very handsome. My aunt and uncle adopted him because they fell in love with me. My gammy—that's my grandmother—says I have the best facial expressions she's ever seen in a dog, and Tyson has the most guilty looking eyes that make you melt. Silly Gammy. I love her!

After reading my story, and understanding that many of my brothers and sisters have been through similar experiences, my hope is that now you will recognize we're not as mean and scary as people say we are. We're just like all other dogs in need of a home filled with love.

Who knows? If enough of you hear about what happened to me, as well as other stories similar to mine, maybe someday the world will again see us the way it did years ago. People will remember we're instinctively "nanny dogs," and love us the way we were once loved.

If you're ever sad about something just remember, Pitties are great companions and friends. We will cheer you up and help you find happiness because it's in our blood. We'll lick you, let you hug us and rub our bellies, and we'll make you laugh. I promise.

Life is precious, and it's supposed to be fun and enjoyable. Let's all do our best to have happier, healthier lives, sharing our joy and love with a companion who will give even more love in return.

My dad was the one who encouraged me to share my story. He's an author who also wrote a book sharing his unique story. I think mine is funnier and better, but don't tell him that. He can be competitive and hates losing. If you get a chance to read his book, *The World Through my Dyslexic Eyes: Battling Learning Disabilities, Depression, and Finding*

*Purpose,* just tell him you liked my book best and see how he reacts.

Dad and Mom are also working on another book about Pit Bulls, and I think it's a good idea. These days all people hear are the bad stories about my breed. It's important for everyone to hear the positive stories, too. This is what we are trying to change together as a family.

I enjoyed talking with you all. My best advice today: Don't judge others and always be nice. You never know what someone, including a dog, has been through, or how they've been mistreated in the past. Your kind voice and gentle hands will go a long way in showing them that there is good in our world today.

I hope you all have a Bullyful day! Have fun and be safe. Remember if you ever need a great companion and sidekick, a Pit Bull is the way to go. We'll be your best friend for life.

Did you adopt one of my brothers or sisters yet? No? Well, what are you waiting for? Put my book down and go find a new best friend. You can share my story with your parents and help them to also realize how special having a companion like me will be for your whole family.

Wait! What's that? I hear that jingling noise coming up the road outside. Is that what I think it is? It is! The ice cream truck is on its way! Sorry, kids, but I have to go. I have to find my parents and let them know it's time for a tasty treat!

Thanks for listening and tagging along with me.

Love,

Bella Louise Harrower

P.S. By the way, that's my real paw print.

# ACKNOWLEDGMENTS

I hope you enjoyed my book and reading about my life. However, it wasn't just me and my awesome parents who made this book become a reality. We had a lot of help while working on it.

I'd like to begin by thanking my two aunts, Jen and Megan. Jen edited all the pictures inside the book, and Megan runs FernandFeatherPhotography.com. She did my glamour photo shoot so we'd have great pictures of me for the cover.

To my cousins, Michael, Sara, Teagan, Ray, Timmy, and Charlotte, thank you for reading my book during its draft stages to make sure my story will be enjoyable for other kids.

Elizabeth, our amazing editor, thank you for being with us on this journey. You have selflessly poured your heart and soul into our message, and we are honored that you share our passion and love for animals. We have enjoyed getting to know you, and we couldn't have done it without your support and encouragement.

Elizabeth is also a writer. You can find her work at ElizabethCourtright.com and on Amazon. All proceeds from her books benefit the Third Chance Foundation, a non-profit scholarship fund for foster and adopted kids. You can find out more at ThirdChanceFound.org.

Brian, Elizabeth's husband, was a huge help with the cover. Thank you, Brian, for all the amazing graphic design. We really appreciate it.

To the rest of our family: Thank you for your support and prayers throughout this journey. We appreciate all of your love over the last few months while we have been diligently working to make this book become a reality. Most of all, thank you for being a Pittie loving family!

# Connecting

Did you enjoy this book? If you did, would you be willing to share a review on Amazon? Reviews help books like Bella's to be seen by other readers. Help us make her story, and the plight of many unfortunate Pit Bulls, known to the world.

More information can be found at:

PeterHarrower.com

Or

Please feel free to reach out to Peter at:

harrower623@gmail.com

Peter Harrower's other book,
*The World Through My Dyslexic Eyes*
is also available on Amazon.